The Laugh Stand

ADVENTURES IN HUMOR

Brian P. Cleary

Illustrations by J. P. Sandy

M MILLBROOK PRESS · MINNEAPOLIS

To Mike and Ryan —B.P.C.
To Joyce, Eric, and Michael —J.P.S.

Text copyright © 2008 by Brian P. Cleary
Illustrations copyright © 2008 by Lerner Publishing Group, Inc.

Millbrook Press
A division of Lerner Publishing Group, Inc.
241 First Avenue North
Minneapolis, MN 55401 U.S.A.

Website address: www.lernerbooks.com

Library of Congress Cataloging-in-Publication Data

Cleary, Brian P., 1959—
    The laugh stand : adventures in humor / by Brian P. Cleary ; illustrated by J.
P. Sandy.
        p.   cm.
    ISBN 978—0—8225—7849—9 (lib. bdg. : alk. paper)
    1. American wit and humor. 2. Play on words. I. Title.
PN6165.C62 2008
817—dc22   2007021889

Manufactured in the United States of America
1 2 3 4 5 6 — DP — 13 12 11 10 09 08

APR 2 2 2008

TABLE OF CONTENTS

ANAGRAM CRACKERS

Anagrams take the letters in a word, phrase, or sentence and by rearranging them, create another word, phrase, or sentence.

SAINT can become

SATIN or **STAIN**.

GERMAN becomes **MANGER**.

All the words formed from colored blocks in the following sentences are anagrams of other words in the same sentence:

PANS always **SNAP** my dad's **NAPS**.

As **RHEA'S** preparing to **SHEAR**, she **HEARS** the **HARES** as they **SHARE** secrets.

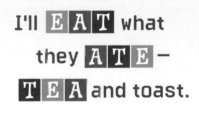

I'll **EAT** what they **ATE** — **TEA** and toast.

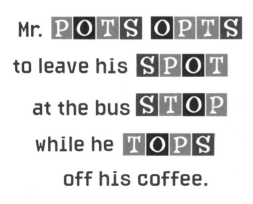

Mr. **POTS OPTS** to leave his **SPOT** at the bus **STOP** while he **TOPS** off his coffee.

The **DANGER**
in the **GRANDE**
GARDEN
RANGED
from high to low
for the
GANDER.

EMIL'S SMILE
is still there after walking
through **MILES**
of the **SLIME**
of **LIMES**.

ELVIS sells **VEILS** and **LEVI'S** and preaches against **EVILS** to anyone who **LIVES** close by.

And check out this anagram sentence:

WAS SHE THE STAR ON THIS TOUR?

THE RAT HASH STEW IS NOT SOUR.

CURL UP AND DIAGRAM

In this section, I have tried to include many different types of words in these short verses. My challenge was to write a rhyming piece that included at least one noun, verb, adjective, pronoun, preposition, and adverb—as well as pairs of words that are synonyms, antonyms, homonyms, and homophones. I even threw in a simile (a figure of speech comparing two unlike things, usually linked by the word "like" or "as") just to show off.

Try showing off a little yourself. I've only coded one example of each type of word. There are more examples of most of them, and I've used articles, conjunctions, and contractions as well. See how many words you can categorize. Watch for words such as "quickly" that have more than one category. You'll find all the words identified in the answer key on page 44.

WORDS

Whether they're chosen
quite slowly or quickly,
hastily scribbled or
lettered quite slickly,
they tell us the news that
the gnus have new shoes.
Without 'em our language
would sure be a snooze!

CAT-ATONIC

When Mr. Foley slowly

moved his roly-poly cat,

he found eight kittens,

small as mittens,

beneath her roll of fat!

Four shy, four bold,

the tiny fold would roll

and squirm and play

while mother ate,

and tried to sleep,

for she'd had quite a day.

Noun: a person, place, or thing	**Synonyms:** words having the same or nearly the same meaning as each other
Verb: expresses action, occurrence, or existence	**Antonyms:** words meaning the opposite of each other
Adjective: describes a noun or pronoun	**Homonyms:** words that are pronounced the same and spelled the same but have different meanings
Pronoun: used in place of a noun or noun phrase	
Preposition: shows relationship of one word to another	**Homophones:** words that are pronounced the same but have different spellings and different meanings
Adverb: modifies a verb, adjective, or other adverb	

TOM SWIFTIES

are a special type of pun, usually involving what is known as an adverb of manner. Read a few, and see if you get them.

"This sure is flat land," Tom said **plainly**.

"These are my underpants," Tom said **briefly**.

"Why didn't you tell me it
was a piranha tank?"
Tom asked **offhandedly**.

"Stop! Thief!"
Tom said **arrestingly**.

"I've just washed my bedroom
window," Tom said **clearly**.

"These hot dogs are tasty,"
Tom said **frankly**.

"America's national
bird looks sick,"
Tom said **illegally**.

"My mom cut too much hair off,"
Tom said, **distressed**.

"My shirt doesn't have any buttons," Tom **snapped**.

"These scissors are dull," Tom said **bluntly**.

"My clothes are all wrinkled," Tom said, **depressed**.

"I've never had an accident," Tom said **recklessly**.

"I'm a lousy banjo player," Tom **fretted**.

"It's poison ivy," Tom said **rashly**.

"I love camping,"
Tom said **intently**.

"I failed my exam,"
Tom said **testily**.

"Here is your gift,"
Tom said **presently**.

"I inherited this,"
Tom said **willfully**.

"I've been in the doctor's
waiting room all morning,"
Tom said **patiently**.

"I got my knee brace off on
Monday, not Tuesday," said Tom,
standing corrected.

THE OBFUSCATION STATION

Obfuscation means "to make difficult the understanding or perception of something, usually written or spoken." It is intended to confuse, or even to hide or mask what is truly meant in a statement, often by using big fancy-schmancy words. Take a look at these phrases, and see if you can decode the simple rhyming sentence that lies beneath the pile of extra verbiage. If you need help, turn to the answer key on page 45.

The member of a ship's crew requires a human being whose occupation involves the alteration of outer garments.

The mongrel canine descended on to the back of his hip that forms the fleshy part of his backside.

There is a dried piece of mucus from the nasal cavity in the sweet, refined sucrose product.

My academic instructor was someone who made a piercing, shrill, high-pitched sound.

The one who is perpetually smiling, along with the one who creates animal pelts and hides for profit, and the victorious one came together to consume an evening meal.

SHORT STUFF

Unlike the verbosity of "The Obfuscation Station," this section, through double meaning or rhyme, celebrates in brief form the wit and wackiness of words.

Overheard at a cookout: "Frank Furter, meat Patty."

Snowman cop to snowman thief: "Freeze!"

An introduction on the Ark: "Noah, boa. Boa, Noah."

Veterinarian to dog with broken leg: "Heal."

The entire *Caveman Cookbook*: "Heat meat."

SPELL-CZECH

Because English is made up of words from several languages (Latin, German, Greek, French, among others), we have lots of different ways to pronounce the very same letters. It's been said that this set of letters **GHOTI** could spell "fish." How? Take the "**GH**" from cough. Take the "**O**" from women. Take the "**TI**" from nation. F-I-SH, right? Using the chart below, see if you can figure out some of the words on the opposite page. If you need help, see the answer key on page 45.

Letters...	...From the word...	...Sound like
BT	debt	t
CHET	ricochet	shay
CI	delicious or gracious	sh
E	risqué	long a
EAU	bureau	long o
EIGH	eight, neighbor	long a
F	of	v
GH	cough	f
GN	gnu	n
I	handicap	long e
MB	limb or climb	m
MN	hymn, column	m
O	women	short i
OUGH	through	long u
OUGH	bough (tree branch)	ow
PH	phone	f
PT	pterodactyl	t
TI	lotion, notion	sh
U	bury	short e

TIOUGHBT

CIEAU

GHEIGHMN

GNEIGHMN

MBOBTPTUGN

Try building your own "Spell-Czech" creations!

THE FUNNY PAPERS

Cartoons are drawings, often coupled with words, designed to entertain, make a political statement, or poke fun at the way things are in the world around us. This form of humor and satire first became popular throughout Great Britain and the United States in the 1800s.

"We don't have one."

"Right now, my dad is trying
to fix somebody's sink with my
peanut butter and jelly."

"Oh, let me guess—
you need a referee again!"

"There's nothing quite like nature."

"Good news!
We're invited to a brunch!"

"No Melvin, a chalkboard doesn't have spell-check."

The real reason police in Great Britain wear those hats.

POETRY BY NUMBERS

Ever notice that 8 is phonetically identical to ate, or that 2 sounds just like to, or too? Understanding these poems requires you to do a little math and to substitute the number that sounds just like the word (like for or won). If you need help, see the answer key on page 46.

Remembering Grandpa Joe

My Grandpa Joe
came by each day
(10 – 6) coffee
or (20 X 2),

(12 - 10) play some
cards or checkers
with my mother
or with me.

On days when
he had (9 - 8),
he used (25 - 23)
celebrate and dance,

And every time
he (40 + 40)
had to loosen
up his pants.

urp!

I've Got Your Number

Sweeter than
some pie I (2 X 4),
you're funny,
smart, and kind.

You're heavenly
(10 ÷ 5) look at,
and you're off (50 ÷ 5)
on my mind.

You're prettier
than Erin, Caitlin,
Stephanie, and Kath.

Are you the
perfect (10 - 9) (2 X 2) me?
Well, honey, do the math.

POETRY OF NOTE

We've played with words and numbers—and now it is music's turn to provide some mirth. Just as we use letters to spell out words, musicians use symbols to tell a piano player, for instance, which of the eighty-eight keys to play. And the cool thing about this language is that it's the same for everybody, no matter what language (German, French, Chinese, for example) they speak! Use the key at the bottom of this page to decode the little musical puzzles that appear here and there in the following poems.

Each of those notes corresponds to a letter, which will help you turn those dots into real words! Hop to it, maestro! If you need help, see the answer key on page 46.

All the poems use the treble clef as shown below. (Notes in the bass clef are different.)

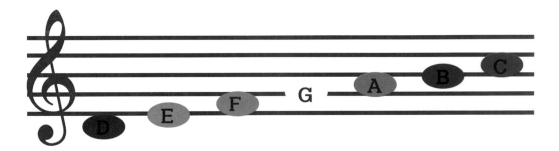

MY BEAUTIFUL VOICE

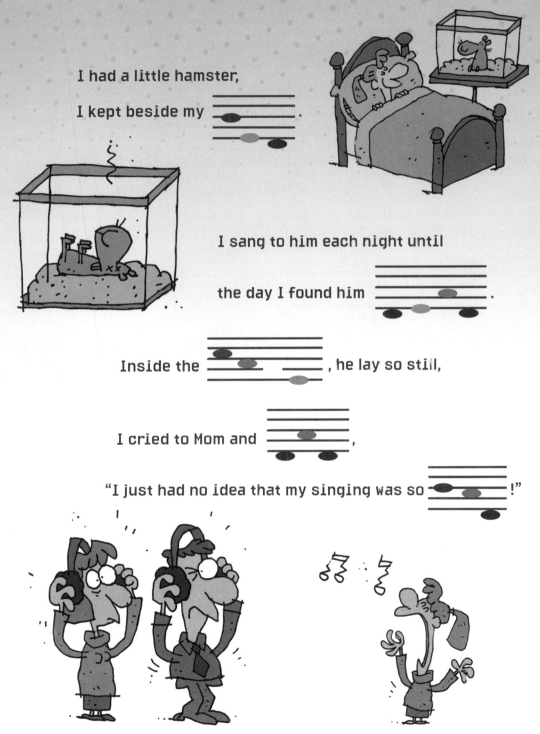

I had a little hamster,

I kept beside my ___ .

I sang to him each night until

the day I found him ___ .

Inside the ___ , he lay so still,

I cried to Mom and ___ ,

"I just had no idea that my singing was so ___ !"

27

A DRIVING FORCE

Always fashion conscious,

my older sister, Madge,

quit her police force job because

her purse clashed with her ▬▬▬▬ .

Then she started waitressing

at ▬▬▬▬ and Joe's ▬▬▬▬ .

She'd ▬▬▬▬ with guys who had no cash,

and ▬▬▬▬ them anyway.

She drove them crazy in ▬▬ shop,

a library, and lab.

She drove them nuts at lifeguarding,

so now she drives a ▬▬▬▬ .

THE GAG BAG

At Halloween, my [♪] will never

hand out gum or sweets.

Each trick-or-treater's [♪] just falls

when first they see our "treats."

Each [♪] receives some [♪], an [♪],

or corn, but never candy.

"Whatever's in the fridge," he'll [♪],

"whatever food is handy."

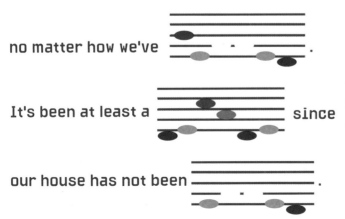

Each Halloween it's been the same,

no matter how we've [♪].

It's been at least a [♪] since

our house has not been [♪].

29

PLURALS OF WIDSOM

English is one crazy language. Most of the time, when you want to refer to more than one of something (like bugs, scabs, worms, or scary-looking clowns), all you have to do is add an "s" on the end of the word and you make it plural. There are exceptions, however. These are called irregular plurals because adding an "s" doesn't make them plural, it just makes them sound kind of silly. Just take a look. Do you know of any more?

You won't find any gooses
At the park or on the beach.
And tooths cannot be found
In any dental class they teach.

"Foots" is not the word for
What belongs inside your shoes.
And if you bet that "oxes"
Is a word, you're gonna lose.

You'll never find three mans
On any billboard, ad, or mural,
So simply adding "s," it seems,
Won't always make things plural.

Now, if there's more than just one goose,
Then what you've got are geese.
But don't deduce that many moose
Would then be called some meese.

And what about the ox? You'll find
The plural word is *oxen*.
But if two foxes do their wash,
Are foxen cleaning soxen?

Without the proper dental care,
Our mouths would just be mush.
And since we don't have just one tooth,
Why isn't it a teethbrush?

POTS AND PANGRAMS

PANGRAMS are sentences that use each of the twenty-six letters of the alphabet at least once. When you get the hang of it, see if you can write one that's fewer than sixty letters long. I even tried a pangram rhyming verse.

My cat, Sphinx, walked very quickly by the cage of jaguars at the zoo.

Zack, have you watched Bud's juvenile oxen quarrel in my fig patch?

Vicky's gross cousin, Max, just requested a half-pound bowl of zits.

Alex, Jacqueline, and Buffy pluck their damaged violas with zest.

Six very polite hogs
want fruit, black jam,
quiche, and jazz.

Jack and William
have a quirky
zebra-print box
of eggs.

My mom said vexed—and quite perplexed,
"Your bedroom's such a junk shed—
With pizza, slews of games, and shoes,
I cannot find your bunk bed!"

Daffynitions

These are silly, made-up definitions that sound almost like they're real! Most are puns or rely on your examining (sometimes out loud) each of the syllables before you really get the little verbal joke. I'll bet you can think of one or two of these yourself!

Benign: This is what you are after you be eight.

Elixir: What my dog does to my sister

Cartoons: The musical selections one hears while in an automobile

Gulf wind: The young lady that a boy takes on dates, such as to movies or dances, as in "Mom and Dad, this is my gulf wind, Webecca."

Inverse: How Dr. Seuss wrote most of his books

Claustrophobic: A person with an irrational fear of Santa

Gladiator: What my cat was after getting ahold of my parakeet

Door key: This describes how the principals at most schools usually dress.

Border: What my brother did to the girl he was recently dating

Journey: The thing you skin or scrape when you fall off jour bike

Marooned: This describes the survivors of a collision involving two ships—one carrying a cargo of brown paint, and the other carrying a cargo of red paint.

Pink carnation: This is what we would be if everyone in our country drove an automobile that was a particular shade of pale red.

Denial: A river in Egypt

Broker: What I accidentally did to my sister's favorite doll

USE YOUR HEADLINES

English is a tricky language. A missing hyphen or comma, coupled with the fact that our words often have two or more meanings, can turn an otherwise straightforward message into something confusing, amusing, and sometimes a little dark. See if you can figure out the original meaning of these headlines, and what would have to be changed in order to be more a little more clear (and a lot less funny). Once you get the hang of it, try a few yourself.

THE SUMM TIMES

JURORS HEAR ALLIGATOR BITE EXPERT

...I wonder if he was screaming?

THE WHATABIG MESSENGER

MISSING EVIDENCE FOUND BY FLOWERPOT

...pretty smart flowerpot!

THE HALL MONITOR

SOCCER STAR SENDS SHOT OFF HEAD THROUGH GOAL IN FINAL SECONDS

...how many points do you get for that?

DAILY SNOOZE

ONE IN FIFTEEN NEW ENGLANDERS LIVES ON WATER

GLUG
GLUG
GLUG

...don't you think they'd get hungry?!

The Broken Record

SCHOOL BOARD
WILL RULE ON PLAYGROUND

. . . they're adults, of course they rule.

THE IRONON DISPATCH

INJURED
PLAYER
TO BE SEEN
BY 8 FOOT
SPECIALISTS

. . . sure, they're tall, but are they good doctors?

... where can
I get a job
like that?

... depending on
the food, I guess.

ANSWER KEY

CURL UP AND DIAGRAM, PAGES 8–9

WORDS

Adjective: new

Adverb: slowly, hastily, slickly, quite, sure

Antonym: slowly/quickly

Article: the, a

Conjunction: or, whether

Contraction: they're, 'em

Homophone: news/gnus

Noun: words, news, gnus, shoes, language, snooze

Preposition: without

Pronoun: they, us, that, 'em, our

Synonym: hastily/quickly

Verb: chosen, scribbled, lettered, tell, have, would, be

CAT-ATONIC

Adjective: roly-poly, eight, small, four, shy, bold, tiny

Adverb: slowly, as, quite

Antonyms: shy/bold

Article: the, a

Conjunction: when, while, and, for

Contraction: she'd

Homonyms: roll/roll

Homophones: eight/ate, four/for

Noun: Mr. Foley, cat, kittens, mittens, roll, fat, fold, mother, day

Preposition: beneath, of

Pronoun: he, her, she

Simile: small as mittens

Synonyms: small/tiny

Verb: moved, found, would, roll, squirm, play, ate, tried, to sleep, had

THE OBFUSCATION STATION, PAGES 14–15

Page 14, top — The sailor needed a tailor.

Page 14, bottom — The mutt fell on his butt.

Page 15, top — The booger is in the sugar.

Page 15, center — My teacher was a screecher.

Page 15, bottom — The grinner, the skinner, and
the winner met for dinner.

SPELL-CZECH, PAGES 18–19

TIOUGHBT = Shoot (the TI from lotion, the OUGH from through,
the BT from debt)

CIEAU = Show (the CI from delicious, the EAU from bureau)

GHEIGHMN = Fame (the GH from cough, the EIGH from
neighbor, the MN from column)

GNEIGHMN = Name (the GN from sign, the EIGH from eight, the
MN from hymn)

MBOBTPTUGN = Mitten (the MB from limb, the O from women,
the BT from debt, the PT from pterodactyl, the U from
bury, the GN from gnu)

POETRY BY NUMBERS PAGE 24-25

REMEMBERING GRANDPA JOE

My Grandpa Joe came by each day
(10 – 6 = 4) four/for coffee or (20 X 2 = 40) forty/for tea,
(12 – 10 = 2) two/to play some cards or checkers
with my mother or with me.
On days when he had (9 – 8 = 1) one/won,
he used (25 – 23 = 2) two/to celebrate and dance,
and every time he (40 + 40 = 80) eighty/ ate he
had to loosen up his pants.

I'VE GOT YOUR NUMBER

Sweeter than some pie I (2 X 4 = 8) eight/ate,
you're funny, smart, and kind.
You're heavenly (10 ÷ 5 = 2) two/to look at,
and you're off (50 ÷ 5 = 10) ten (off-ten/often) on my mind.
You're prettier than Erin, Caitlin,
Stephanie, and Kath.
Are you the perfect (10 – 9 = 1) one/one (2 X 2 = 4) four/for me?
Well, honey, do the math.

POETRY OF NOTE PAGE 26-29

MY BEAUTIFUL VOICE
I had a little hamster,
I kept beside my BED.
I sang to him each night until
the day I found him DEAD.
Inside the CAGE, he lay so still,
I cried to Mom and DAD,
"I just had no idea
that my singing was so BAD!"

A DRIVING FORCE

Always fashion conscious,
my older sister, Madge,
quit her police force job because
her purse clashed with her **BADGE**.
Then she started waitressing
at **ED** and Joe's **CAFÉ**.
She'd **GAB** with guys who had no cash,
and **FEED** them anyway.
She drove them crazy in **A** shop,
a library, and lab.
She drove them nuts at lifeguarding,
so now she drives a **CAB**.

THE GAG BAG

At Halloween, my **DAD** will never
hand out gum or sweets.
Each trick-or-treater's **FACE** just falls
when first they see our "treats."
Each **BAG** receives some **BEEF**, an **EGG**,
or corn, but never candy.
"Whatever's in the fridge," he'll **ADD**,
"whatever food is handy."
Each Halloween it's been the same,
no matter how we've **BEGGED**.
It's been at least a **DECADE** since
our house has not been **EGGED**.

FURTHER READING

Agee, Jon. *Elvis Lives!: and Other Anagrams*. New York: Farrar, Straus and Giroux, 2004.

Cleary, Brian P. *Rhyme and PUNishment: Adventures in Wordplay.* Minneapolis: Millbrook Press, 2006.

Lederer, Richard. *The Circus of Words: Acrobatic Anagrams, Parading Palindromes, Wonderful Words on a Wire, and More Lively Letter Play*. Chicago: Chicago Review Press, 2001.

Rosen Michael, *Walking the Bridge of Your Nose: Wordplay Poems Rhymes*. New York: Kingfisher, 1999.

Steig, William. *CDB!*. Rev ed. New York: Aladdin, 2005.

Steig, William. *CDC?* Rev ed. New York: Farrar, Straus and Giroux, 2003.

WEBSITES

Ahajokes.com
http://www.ahajokes.com/funny_cartoons.html
Hundreds of cartoons are arranged by topic (animals, food, computer, sports, etc.). And you can also access them through a keyword search.

Anagramsite.com
http://www.anagramsite.com/
This site allows you to enter a word or phrase, and a list of possible anagrams will appear. Hundreds of anagrams in the categories of sports, celebrities, TV, food and drink, movies, politics, around the world, and miscellaneous are available.

English-Zone.com
http://english-zone.com/spelling/plurals.html
Unusual plural endings are placed in ten categories so that you can see a pattern for each group.

Just Riddles and More. . . !
http://www.justriddlesandmore.com/definitions.html
This site offers an interactive guessing game in which you're given some wacky definitions and are asked to come up with the correct word.

Leaf Publishing
http://www.leafpublishing.com/fracturedheadlines.htm
This site offers some practice at headline writing by allowing you to rearrange words and then illustrate and publish your result. Humor is definitely possible!

Learning Stream
http://www.lifestreamcenter.net/DrB/Lessons/TS/diagram.htm
This online lesson teaches how to diagram a sentence.

The World of Brian P. Cleary
http://www.brianpcleary.com
The author's own website explores a number of ways to have fun with words, numbers, poetry, and more.

The Wordplay Website
http://www.fun-with-words.com/tom_swifties.html
A nice collection of Tom Swifties as well as other categories of wordplay are featured.

The Wordplay Website
http://www.fun-with-words.com/pang_example.html
Pangrams abound at this site. There is a link to the history of pangrams, and you are encouraged to submit your own efforts for display.